A Note to Parents

DK READERS is a compelling program for beginning readers, designed in conjunction with leading literacy experts, including Dr. Linda Gambrell, Distinguished Professor of Education at Clemson University. Dr. Gambrell has served as President of the National Reading Conference, the College Reading Association, and the International Reading Association.

Beautiful illustrations and superb full-color photographs combine with engaging, easy-to-read stories to offer a fresh approach to each subject in the series. Each DK READER is guaranteed to capture a child's interest while developing his or her reading skills, general knowledge, and love of reading.

The five levels of DK READERS are aimed at different reading abilities, enabling you to choose the books that are exactly right for your child:

Pre-level 1: Learning to read
Level 1: Beginning to read
Level 2: Beginning to read alone
Level 3: Reading alone
Level 4: Proficient readers

The "normal" age at which a child begins to read can be anywhere from three to eight years old. Adult participation through the lower levels is very helpful for providing encouragement, discussing storylines, and sounding out unfamiliar words.

No matter which level you select, you can be sure that you are helping your child learn to read, then read to learn!

LONDON, NEW YORK, MUNICH,
MELBOURNE, AND DELHI

Series Editor Deborah Lock
U.S. Editor John Searcy
Senior Art Editor Sonia Whillock-Moore
Production Editor Siu Chan
Production Pip Tinsley
Jacket Designer Sonia Whillock-Moore
Photographer Andy Crawford
Production Photographer Keith Pattison

Reading Consultant
Linda Gambrell, Ph.D.

First American Edition, 2008
08 09 10 11 12 10 9 8 7 6 5 4 3 2 1
Published in the United States by DK Publishing
375 Hudson Street, New York, New York 10014

DK books are available at special discounts when purchased in bulk for
sales promotions, premiums, fund-raising, or educational use.
For details, contact: DK Publishing Special Markets
375 Hudson Street, New York, New York 10014
SpecialSales@dk.com

A catalog record for this book is available
from the Library of Congress
ISBN: 978-0-7566-3490-2 (Paperback)
ISBN: 978-0-7566-3491-9 (Hardcover)

Color reproduction by Colourscan, Singapore
Printed and bound in China by L. Rex Printing Co. Ltd.

The publisher wishes to thank Cavan Day-Lewis,
Caroline Day-Lewis and Stewart Cairns.
The production of *Flat Stanley* featured was produced by West
Yorkshire Playhouse and Polka Theatre in 2006–7. Based on the
story by Jeff Brown with illustrations by Scott Nash and adapted for
the stage by Mike Kenny. It was directed by Gail McIntyre, designed
by Karen Tennent, lighting design by Ian Scott, animation by
John Barber, composition by Julian Ronnie and sound design by
Martin Pickersgill. The original cast were Ian Bonar, Stewart
Cairns, Lisa Howard, and Robin Simpson.
Flat Stanley is published by Egmont in the UK
and by HarperCollins in the United States.
With thanks also to all at Polka Theatre, Wimbledon, London,
www.polkatheatre.com, including Chris Barham, James Cartwright,
Anwen Cooper, Hélène Hill, Tim Highman, Paula Hopkins, Anne
James, Kim Kish, Ben Powell-Williams, and Mary Trafford.
Flat Stanley illustration © Scott Nash
The publisher would like to thank the following for their kind
permission to reproduce their photographs:
a=above, b=below/bottom, c=center, l=left, r=right, t=top
Alamy Images: Frank Chmura 32. **Flickr.com:**
vancouverfringephotos 24-25b. **Kenneth A. Goldberg:** 30t;
All other images © Dorling Kindersley
For more information see: www.dkimages.com

Discover more at
www.dk.com

DK READERS

A Trip to the Theater

Written by Deborah Lock

DK Publishing

All morning, Jake was
very excited.
"I can't wait to see
Uncle Stewart
in his play today,"
Jake told his mom
for the third time.

Jake's uncle was an actor
in a theater group.
The group travels
around the country,
performing in theaters.

After lunch, Jake and his mom
went to the theater to meet Stewart.
Stewart was going to take
them on a tour of
the backstage area,
before they watched
the play.

As they arrived,
Jake looked up at
the theater's large sign.
All around the entrance,
there were posters
that showed the dates
and times of the performances.

Jake eagerly pushed open
the doors and stepped into
the theater lobby.
His mom went to the box office
to buy two tickets for the play.

Then Stewart came to meet them.
"Hello, Jake," said Stewart
with a beaming smile.
"Welcome to the theater.
Let me show you around."

"I'll show you the auditorium first," said Stewart, leading the way. "This is where you'll sit to watch our performance."

"Wow, it's big," Jake gasped, as he looked at all the seats.

"Yes, there are 300 seats," explained Stewart.

"At the top is the control room where the sound-and-lighting operator sits during the play."

Stage lighting

Lights shine onto the actors on stage. Different shades and colors help change the mood of a play.

"The stage is set up for my favorite scene," said Stewart. "This is the park where my character flies his kite."

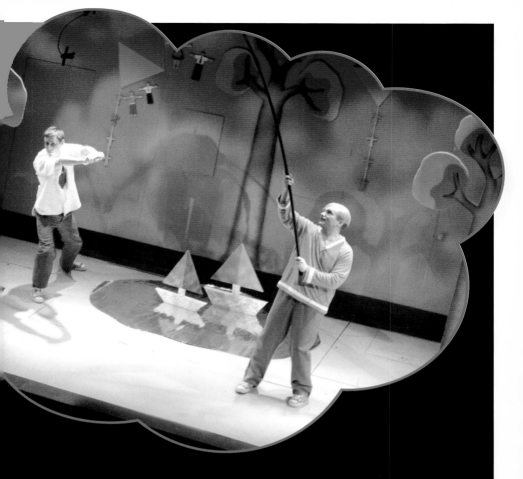

"What are the trees, kites, and boats made from?" asked Jake. "Just painted wood and paper," said Stewart. "Let's go backstage and I'll show you where they were made."

Stewart led Jake and his mom through a door into the backstage area. "This is the workshop," said Stewart. "Our prop manager, Ben, makes the scenery and props here." "What are props?" asked Jake. "They are the objects that actors use on stage," said Stewart.

Fake food

Food props are often made from foam, clay, wire mesh, or paper, and then painted to look real.

15

"Next, I'll show you where our costumes are made," said Stewart. They entered a room full of colorful clothes, hats, wigs, and jewelry. "This is Sue," said Stewart. "She designs the costumes we wear in our plays."

"Would you like to try on this police officer's costume?" Sue asked Jake. "Yes, please," replied Jake. Jake laughed at his reflection in the mirror.

Costume designer

Costumes are based on sketches drawn by the costume designer. She chooses the styles and fabrics to suit the play.

"Now let's take a look at the area behind the stage," said Stewart. As they walked downstairs, they met James, the director. "Hi, Stewart," said James. "Are you ready for the show? The final rehearsal went really well yesterday." "What's a rehearsal?" asked Jake. "It's a practice performance of the play," explained Stewart.

Director

The director oversees every part of the play. He helps everyone work together to make the show a success.

It was very dark behind the stage.
"This is Chris, the stage manager,"
said Stewart.
"What are you doing?" asked Jake.
"I'm making sure that all the props
and costumes are in the right
place," replied Chris.
"We need to know exactly where
they are so that we
can find them quickly
during the play,"
added Stewart.

Stage manager
The stage manager
makes sure everything is
running smoothly during
the performance, both
onstage and backstage.

"In this show, some of the actors play more than one character," explained Chris.
"They have to change quickly from one costume to another."

"The actor who plays the father also plays a doctor, a security guard, and a policeman!" Stewart added.

"I'll look out for him in the play," said Jake.

"If we hurry, we'll have time to see the control room," said Stewart. "Follow me."

"This is Abby, the operator," said Stewart, as they entered the control room. "During the performance, she uses the control panel to change the lighting and create sound effects."

"I have to follow the script carefully so I don't miss my cue," said Abby.

"It's time for me to get ready,"
said Stewart, checking his watch.

"Come and see my
dressing room," said Stewart.
They entered a room filled with
mirrors surrounded by bright lights.
"I sit here to put on my makeup,"
explained Stewart.

"We should go find our seats," said Jake's mom. "Good luck, Stewart." "Sometimes people say 'break a leg' instead of 'good luck' to actors before a show," explained Stewart. "Break a leg," laughed Jake.

"Now it's time to get into character," thought Stewart. He started to put on his makeup.

"I think I need more color on my chin," he said.

Next, he painted his lips
and cheeks a rosy red
and added black freckles
with a thin paintbrush.
Finally, Stewart pinned
on his orange wig.
"Perfect!" he said.
He put on his costume
and headed off to the stage.

Meanwhile, Jake and his mom were sitting in the auditorium, surrounded by chattering people. Suddenly, the lights faded, the audience stopped talking, and the music began. The play was about the adventures of a boy, who was played by Stewart.

Mom bought Jake some candy during the intermission.
In the second half, Stewart's character caught a burglar.
It was very exciting.
At the end, the actors bowed to the audience.
Jake clapped very loudly.
"That was fantastic!" he said.

THE END

Theater Facts

The ancient Greeks performed their plays in large outdoor theaters called amphitheaters. The actors wore masks to represent their characters.

Medieval plays were first performed on wagons in large outdoor marketplaces.

Later, open-air playhouses were built. Audiences sat or stood on three sides of the stage. Hardly any scenery was used.

During the 17th and 18th centuries, plays were performed in fully lit rooms. The stage had a decorative frame around it.

Today, audiences sit in the dark, watching the performance on a lit stage. Plays may have lots of scenery and special effects. Some famous plays are made into movies.